MW01230619

The

Christmas

Star

By Peter Caligiuri
ISBN: 9798358736801

The Christmas Star

ISBN# 979-8358909281

by Peter Caligiuri © 2022

All Creatures Mostly Small publishing
Showing our Big God in the Smallest Details of Life

Scripture quotations from KJV and The Holy Bible, English Standard Version. ESV® Text Edition: 2016. Copyright © 2001 by Crossway Bibles, a publishing ministry of Good News Publishers.

This Book Belongs To

_____

Presented by

_____

The Christmas Star

A star burns bright a billion years
Before its rays grow dim
A sparrow lives just two or three
And yet God cares for him

But before the dawn of time
God's candle lit the night
And came for us at Bethlehem
When shepherds, saw His light

Now to our hiding place He comes
At doors that we've kept locked
To bring HIs light to our dark home
When we open at His knock

Now when Jesus was born in Bethlehem of Judaea in the days of Herod the king, behold, there came wise men from the east to Jerusalem, Saying, Where is he that is born King of the Jews? for we have seen his star in the east, and are come to worship him.
Matthew 1:1-2 KJV

Introduction

For most of us, December 25th is the day we think of as Christmas. But in my home city, with a large population of Ukrainians and Russians, many people mark January 7th as their day of celebration. Sadly, this year, people who calling themselves Christians in their part of the world are in combat rather than celebration. The poet Longfellow in the midst of the American Civil wrote of times like these when he penned these words, "And in despair I bowed my head; There is no peace on earth," * But, were things all that different 2,000 years ago when the wise men saw the star, while Herod plotted murder. And when shepherds were hearing angels sing, the Romans were still busy crushing any resistance to their rule in Israel and finding new ways to tax its inhabitants to maintain their empire.

Yet, just as Longfellow found hope, that "God is not dead, nor doth He sleep." we also have reasons to still smile and celebrate. As we turn our hearts towards the Prince of Peace and remember his birth, He will give us joy and a reason to worship even in our world that is filled with suffering. I invite you to join me over this next month as we set aside the tinsel and notions of Santa to turn your heart to God's only Son, Jesus Christ. He was born to be the light in our dark world, and He suffered and died as God's lamb to set us free from our sins. He is our hope, no matter our situation and our salvation, no matter our battle. He is the one before whom shepherds and wise men bowed and God invites us to come to Him, not only at Christmas, but also on every one of our sunniest mornings and in all our darkest nights. We come with hope because Jesus came as the friend of sinners and as Immanuel

– God with us. We have hope because we remember that He loved us enough to come as an innocent child and then showed us the depth of His love on the cross.

> Then pealed the bells more loud and deep:
> "God is not dead, nor doth He sleep;
> The Wrong shall fail,
> The Right prevail,
> With peace on earth, good-will to men.

I Heard the Bells on Christmas Day by Henry Wadsworth Longfellow

Every year I love to put up our Christmas tree and as I hang the ornaments I remember our family and friends who have given these to us over the years. Some are handmade and others store-bought, but all of them remind me of how Christmas linked us all together. These 30 days of Christmas readings are a mixture of my favorite

Bible stories along with precious memories from our own family. This year I also included a few pages for you to add your own favorite Christmas story. This can be your opportunity to share what you have found on your own journey to find Jesus both at Christmas and forever!

*I Heard the Bells on Christmas Day poem by H W Longfellow 1863

Day 1   The Christmas Star

"… behold, there came wise men from the east to Jerusalem, saying, Where is he that is born King of the Jews? for we have seen his star in the east, and are come to worship him."
Matthew 2:1b-2 KJV

The story of the wisemen does not start with an explanation of their background, instead it begins with a star. The Bible says that, while they were still far away, they saw a star. We don't know if God spoke directly to them, or if it was simply from their understanding of the Hebrew scriptures, but somehow they knew that this star signaled the birth of a special king. Then they made the biggest decision of their lives by le everything behind to follow the star.

Where the wise men came from remains a mystery, but who they were going to see was more important than where they were from.

The same is true for you and me. Some of us might have grown up in broken homes, with difficult, or even dangerous circumstances. Others were born into loving supportive families. But no matter what our background, God has a special purpose for each of us. The wise men knew their purpose, and they were not ashamed to tell everyone. "We have come to worship him." When they finally arrived in Bethlehem, they weren't concerned about their surroundings, nor did they ask why there was no palace for this special king. They simply offered their gifts, bowed before Him, and worshipped at His feet. When the wise men returned home, the star remained behind. That Christmas star still shines, and still leads wise men and women to Jesus who come to worship Him!

Day 2   Doing Big Things For God

Whoever humbles himself like this little child, the same is greatest in the kingdom of heaven.
Matthew 18:4 ESV

The scene of today's verse highlights a day when the disciples were arguing about who was the most important. Maybe it started with. Peter started telling the others how he had walked on water, but then Matthew chimed in by reminding everyone out that he had given Jesus the biggest party. Then in the middle of the commotion, John blurted out, "But he loves me the most!" While their debate raged on, they didn't notice a small child who was listening - but Jesus did. Then Jesus took him by the hand and put him right into the middle and said, "This little child, (who you guys didn't even notice) is the most important one to God.

Haven't we all sometimes lost perspective in the middle of an argument? As the holidays approach do we sometimes get so worked up over the *"big things"* we are doing, that we forget the **"little people"** all around us. When we become so busy doing *"big things"*, we are forgetting that to God there are no big or little things, and no big or little people. What is big to God is whether we are doing the small things that He asks. God will never help us to do what we see as *"big things"*, until we are willing to become like that child who simply wanted to be close to Jesus.

Day 3   A Mother's Faith – Part One

For nothing will be impossible with God." And Mary said, "Behold, I am the servant of the Lord; let it be to me according to your word."
Luke 1:37-38 ESV

You might be surprised to learn that in long-term care facilities, there are also teenagers. Some have had strokes or are in diabetic comas, while some have major disabilities and can no longer be cared for by their families alone. This is the story of one such family that I met in the respiratory ward at Allied Skilled Nursing. It began one day as I was going to visit a friend there and as I passed down the hall, I noticed that in a nearby room lay a teenaged boy with his eyes closed and a woman sitting by his side, holding his hand. So I paused for a minute, cleared my throat, and introduced myself as a volunteer chaplain. She turned to smile, then said,

"Hi, I'm Evelyn (not her real name), this is my son Joey. He's just seventeen." Then she fell silent, so I walked in and sat down, and it wasn't long before she poured out the story of how Joey had gone from being involved in church and being an eagle scout, to experimenting with drugs. Then one night they got the phone call informing them that Joey had overdosed. After several weeks in the hospital, when he still hadn't regained consciousness Joey was transferred to Allied.

"Can I sing him a song?" I asked pointing to my guitar.

"Oh yes please. Joey loves music!" she exclaimed happily. So began the first of many visits, and the first of many prayers for Joey.

Day 4 A Mother's Faith – Part Two

Though Joey's condition didn't seem to change, his mom, just like Mary, believed in God's plan. You see, the Christmas story is not only about God's promise of a Savior, but also about Mary believing that God could do the impossible. The lesson we learn from Evelyn is that even in her despair, she had the unwavering trust that Jesus heard her prayer.

Then one afternoon, when I came to visit, I saw that Joey's eyes were open. He couldn't speak, but he was looking around the room. We prayed again that day, but this time with a greater joy. The following week, Joey was sitting up. His dad had come, and together they were getting ready for Joey to go home. When I walked in with a big smile, Evelyn greeted me enthusiastically, but Joey looked perplexed. "Oh this is Pastor Pete," Evelyn said. He's been coming and praying for you every week. Joey had no memory of me, but he smiled and shook my hand.

"Mom's been telling me about you. Glad to meet you!" he told me. I don't remember them, but I heard about your visits from my parents."

As you read this story about Joey, remember that what matters most to God is our faith. Just like Joey's mom and with Mary, what mattered most was not what other people thought, but what God thinks. He cares for you, and He still answers prayer!

Day 5   Finding Jesus This Christmas

Ask, and it shall be given you; seek, and ye shall find; knock, and it shall be opened unto you: **Matthew 7:7 KJV**

My wife and I used to live in a neighborhood, where the police often closed our street while they broke up fights at the corner bar. One year more than three hundred 911 calls were made because of their clientele. Finally, one night Nany and I decided to do something about it, so we walked to the corner with our prayer group, joined hands outside the bar, and asked God to close it down. Now our request may not sound very spiritual to you, but boy oh boy did our God answer. Just two weeks later our mayor and the chief of police were featured on the local news, standing in front of that bar, and putting a padlock on the door! The bar went up for sale, and new owners came who cleaned up the place and reopened it as a beautiful little restaurant. God had not only heard our prayers, but He also answered with a down to earth practical solution. In this world of gut-wrenching tragedies and mind-boggling changes many of us look to Christmas to restore a sense of normality. But no holiday tradition can give us the solution to our problems. What we find under a Christmas tree or in the laughter of holiday parties is only a temporary and hollow echo of the peace for which our hearts long. What we really need is Jesus Christ. When He tells us to ask Him, seek Him and knock on His door, He also promises to send us answers that we just might see on the local news!

Day 6　To Worship at His Feet

And going into the house, they saw the child with Mary his mother, and they fell down and worshiped him. Then, opening their treasures, they offered him gifts, gold and frankincense and myrrh. **Matthew 2:11 ESV**

One Sunday, at our church our pastor's wife shared a short testimony which ended by her saying, "The more we seek Him: the more He finds us." That little phrase reminded me of the wise men. Sometime after they began their journey, it's goals changed as they went along. They started as emissaries, chosen to carry gifts and give worship to a neighboring king's child. But along the way as they followed the star, it led them further than they could have ever imagined. Maybe when they left Persia, they simply thought it would be an interesting visit to a neighboring kingdom.

But instead of a few days on the road to a nearby destination they discovered that the star led them more than a thousand miles to Israel. When they arrived in Jerusalem, they were invited into the king's palace. The wise men probably unloaded their camels shouting, "Finally we're here!" But that's when things got strange. That evening they were told that the one who they had been seeking was not the king's son, but instead a special chosen one of God, whom the Jews called the Messiah. The next day as they started towards Bethlehem, the star they had followed appeared again and it led them to an ordinary home in a small village. There in the light of God's star they found a child who was the King sent from Heaven. In Him they found the one who had been seeking them and there they opened their treasures and worshiped at His feet!

Day 7   Are You Singing Your Song?

And suddenly there was with the angel a multitude of the heavenly host praising God, and saying, Glory to God in the highest, and on earth peace, good will toward men. **Luke 2:13-14 KJV**

Besides decorated trees, presents, and parties, one thing that sets Christmas apart from other holidays is its songs. In today's verse we read that the angels also had a special song. Not only that but a few verses back, Mary had a song as well as her aunt Elizabeth, and later even those shepherds started singing God's praise. All of these different people became so overwhelmed with the goodness and wonder of God that they simply had to sing!

Today, we no longer have the music or even the instruments that the people used in Bible days.

But even though we don't know what those early Christmas carols sounded like, the Bible tells us every word! God knew that fashions would change, and our styles of music would come and go, but everywhere the story is told, the songs of Christmas are sung. Just as there were songs for Mary and Elizabeth, for those wise men, shepherds and angels, God also has a special song for you. Since it will soon be Christmas, why not start singing your song today?

Day 8   Third Shift Shepherds

And there were in the same country shepherds abiding in the field, keeping watch over their flock by night
Luke 2:8 KJV

When I briefly worked from 11pm till 6 am, I found myself suddenly a part of an exclusive group of people who only see the world from midnight till dawn. On the night that Jesus was born, just above Bethlehem were shepherds who were the third shift workers of their day. The more important shepherds got the first shift jobs. But in the darkness of that night, those unnamed and seemingly unimportant third shift shepherds were about to become the first people on earth to hear the good news of Jesus Christ! That message was that God had remembered His people, He remembered Bethlehem and He even remembered shepherds whom everyone else had forgotten.

Did you ever stop to think that God also remembers you? He is not satisfied to visit only the better homes in the better neighborhoods with the biggest churches with their beautiful appearances. Just as the shepherds were watching their flocks at night so God watches over us when we are going through the darkest moments of our lives. He knows right where we are. He hears us and He still sends angels with His message of good news. There is no better place than right where you are to hear the news; that Jesus Christ came to bring hope and salvation to us all: even to third shift shepherds out in their fields at night!

Day 9 Finding Christmas

And the shepherds returned, glorifying and praising God for all they had heard and seen, as it had been told them.
Luke 2:20 ESV

Mary was chosen for her purity, Joseph for his obedience and the wise men for their gifts, but what could humble shepherds bring? Certainly, most of us would not have picked shepherds to invite to a maternity room, but God did! All they could bring was their humble praise, and for God, that was enough. Their praise echoed in the heart of Mary as the sound of their footsteps vanished into the night and their shouts woke the villagers with good news of great joy! Their very humility lent an authenticity to their message that even wise men's gifts could not bring.

Throughout the life of Jesus, that same humility was seen in the story of a sinful woman's tears washing His feet and a

Samaritan leper who returned to give thanks. We see humility in Mary Magdalene as she waits outside the tomb weeping, while asking where Jesus has gone. In her sorrow Mary failed to recognize Jesus, but when He called her name, she humbly worshipped at His feet. This Christmas Jesus still welcomes simple shepherds, forgiven sinners, and grateful lepers. He is still waiting outside the tomb with the promise that we will find Him when we humbly come to worship.

Day 10
And You Will Call His Name

And behold, you will conceive in your womb and bear a son, and you shall call his name Jesus. **Luke 1:23 ESV**

She will bear a son, and you shall call his name Jesus, for he will save his people from their sins."
Matthew 1:21 ESV

On September 28, 1951, a funny thing happened on the way to the hospital. While my Dad was busy sending a telegram to our family in Italy, telling everyone "Anthony has arrived!" my mom at the last moment decided to name me Peter! Maybe that's why God didn't wait for Joseph and Mary to pick out the name for His Son. God sent them both an advance notice that He must be called Jesus.

As a loving heavenly Father, God saw that what Joseph, Mary, the shepherds, and Wise Men needed was more than anything was the name of a Savior. And the name Jesus means, "Yahweh saves." When our heavenly Father sent us His son, He slipped into our world to reveal Himself in the name of Jesus. In God's plan, Jesus was laid in the manger by Mary, but thirty-three years later He willingly laid His body on the cross to be the Savior who could save us from our sins.

Day 11   God Can Even Use Taxes

And all went to be taxed, everyone into his own city. And Joseph also went up from Galilee, out of the city of Nazareth, into Judaea, unto the city of David, which is called Bethlehem; (because he was of the house and lineage of David :) **Luke 2:3-4 KJV**

There is a great deal of talk in the church about being led by God in our finances, families, and careers. People often talk about God speaking to them about their ministry, buying a house or even choosing a spouse. But amazingly, God chose to lead Mary and Joseph to Bethlehem just in time for Jesus to be born there by having the government send them a bill for taxes!

God's doesn't design His plan to be like a puzzle for us to solve, or a theological issue open to debate. He regularly chooses the most ordinary ways to lead us to some of the most spectacular breakthroughs for our lives. He works that way to show us that He is interested in the everyday concerns of our lives. If He chose to reveal the exact place and time for Jesus' birth by a bill in the mail, we can be confident that if we are willing to obey Him; He will show us the way to go and help us get there right on time!

Day 12   Don't Quit!

And Simon answered, "Master, we toiled all night and took nothing! But at your word I will let down the nets."
Luke 5:5 ESV

Years ago, we had a poster on the wall, of a young boy hunched over on the sidelines of a football game, with the quote, "I quit!" Next to him was another picture - this one of the cross, with the words, "I didn't!"

In spite of our best efforts, we all sometimes come face to face with failure. Maybe you were always the last to get picked for your neighborhood baseball team or today your marriage is struggling, or you don't have a single friend. Whatever failure you are facing, Peter felt the same way after not catching a single fish. But the good news is that Jesus didn't call only the best fishermen, fathers, mothers, or pastors.

He calls all kinds of people, and He doesn't ask us to reach our goals. He asks us to trust Him! When Peter just obeyed and cast his net on the other side of the boat, it got so loaded with fish that it took the efforts of Peter and all his friends to pull it in. But Peter's story is about more than blessings. It is about coming by faith and following Jesus wherever He leads!

And when they had brought their boats to land, they left everything and followed him
Luke 5:11 ESV

Day 13   God's Christmas Music

And suddenly there was with the angel a multitude of the heavenly host praising God and saying, "Glory to God in the highest, and on earth peace among those with whom he is pleased!"
Luke 2:13-14 ESV

My saying with our family, is that "Media and meals don't mix." In other words- no cell phones. But as for music – now that's a different story! Some of my most vivid childhood memories are of my parents playing Beethoven's Ninth symphony or Benny Goodman at suppertime. After 60 years, I can still feel Beethoven's Bababa-boom through my feet and hear the notes of Goodman's clarinet. God invented music long before heaven and earth were created. I think that the first thing He taught the angels was how to sing Holy-Holy-Holy! Jesus sang after the Last Supper and in today's verse David tells us how he loves to sing about God's love and justice. Music is unique among the arts. From ancient Hebrew festivals to 18th century English pubs, songs have resonated while people ate and drank. Music has the power to bring minds and bodies into unity around its melodies and rhythms. So, we need to ask ourselves, "What kind of music are we listening to this Christmas?" Some choose the sounds of football or the rhythm of a reply to a text message. Most public places are filled with generic "Winter Holiday" tunes both new and old. Snowmen and bobsleds are okay with me, but God's Christmas music fills our hearts and minds with grace notes so that our lips can sing His praise!

Day 14   Happy Birthday Jesus

"Where is he who has been born king of the Jews? For we saw his star when it rose and have come to worship him." **Matthew 2:2 ESV**

Long ago we sometimes brought children from our neighborhood to church, including a five-year-old boy named Dylan. Just before Christmas, that year, they had a party at Sunday school, but Dylan wanted nothing to do with it unless one of us went with him. So, I gently took his hand, and we walked down the stairs to the little classroom together. There we sat in a circle on grade school sized chairs as the teacher talked about the Christmas story. Then she passed out cupcakes with a candle for each child.

"Now Jesus was born on Christmas so let's sing happy birthday to Him!"

the teacher said smiling. First, she carefully lit each candle, and then we began to sing. Just as the last note faded Dylan happened to look up at a picture on the wall behind the teacher. There was a painting of Jesus, but not a nativity scene, it was the Last Supper. As he looked closely, Dylan's eyes got bigger and bigger until in excitement he jumped up, pointed to the wall, and shouted,

"Look it's Jesus' birthday party!" Now, thirty years later, I have forgotten all the sermons I heard preached in that church, but the words of Dylan remain in my heart. This Christmas morning as you remember the wise men, shepherds, and angels, also remember Dylan, whose birthday it is, and let's celebrate together!

Day 15 A Word to Remember

And the Word became flesh and dwelt among us, and we have seen his glory, glory as of the only Son from the Father, full of grace and truth.
John 1:14 ESV

When I was in my teens, a friend of mine and I were out late one night in Boston, where we met a street-preacher. He stopped us and with a smile gave us a simple message saying, "I want to tell you about Jesus: That's J-E-S-U-S; Jesus! And He loves you!" That night the power of those words entered my heart and have remained in my memory for 50 years because "Jesus" was the word that I could not forget.

In the Gospel of John, we do not hear a traditional telling of the birth of Jesus. John looks back far earlier than Bethlehem to before the dawn of time and tells us that Jesus was with His

Father till that night in Bethlehem, when the Bible says, "God's Word became flesh."

If Jesus had never come, He would have remained the unspoken word. If the angels had not brought the good news of great joy to the shepherds, how could we know about the comfort and joy He came to bring? But God did speak, Jesus did come, and He remains: the unforgettable Word, who brings salvation for us all!

Day 16   A Cheerful Giver

Each one must give as he has decided in his heart, not reluctantly or under compulsion, for God loves a cheerful giver. **2 Corinthians 9:7 ESV**

When Paul was writing this letter, he was in the middle of his ministry at Ephesus. While Paul remained there for eighteen months he enjoyed remarkable success in preaching the gospel, but he also faced strong opposition culminating with a city-wide riot. According to his detractors his crime was disrespecting the goddess Diana. Paul had been so successful in bringing people to Jesus that many folks who made a living by making images of Diana were losing money. Just as sometimes happens today, they put out malicious misinformation, that resulted in a riot. But Paul, instead of feeling sorry for himself, remained focused on joy. He was determined that no matter the cost he would continue to cheerfully share the gospel. If today, your world seems dark, just remember that Joseph and Mary's reception in Bethlehem was also cold, and dark. No one knew or understood the value of the gift that lay in Mary's arms. But then God gave a joyful message to the shepherds, guided wise men by a shining star and entrusted Mary with the treasure of His only Son. In all these things, God chose to give cheerfully. Why shouldn't we be cheerful givers too?

Day 17   An Upside-Down World

And she brought forth her firstborn son, and wrapped him in swaddling clothes, and laid him in a manger, because there was no room for them in the inn.
Luke 2:7 KJV

It is hard to believe that because of Covid, fourteen months passed by without being able to visit the nursing homes in our area. The area of the building where we had held services was turned into an isolation ward and life as we knew it was turned upside down. When I read today's verse I was reminded that the world of Mary and Joseph was also upside down. Joseph had extra taxes to pay from his meager salary and a very pregnant Mary had to travel ninety miles over dirt roads to Bethlehem. Then at the end of their long journey they discovered that no one was willing to take them in.

But God provided a place, an angel, and a song for them on that lonely night in the stable. He hadn't forgotten about Joseph and Mary and He hasn't forgotten us. His love makes a way even in our most difficult situations. Just as God used shepherds to turn that musty stable into a place of worship so He can transform our most upside-down circumstances into blessings and by His grace turn our world right side up again!

Day 18   One Stitch at a Time

For you formed my inward parts; You knitted me together in my mother's womb. **Psalms 139:13 ESV**

My Mom loved to knit and year after year, stitch by stitch she made beautiful blankets, sweaters, and socks. So, when the Bible tells us that God knit us together, it reminds me of my mother's patient stitching and how she knitted one creation after another. I picture God carefully winding our tiny strands of DNA together to form us, one stitch at a time. When the Bible tells us that Jesus was made just like us, we might think it means that He looked like other men. But it also means that when Gabriel first came to Mary, to tell her she would conceive by the Holy Spirit, that God began knitting Jesus, just as He knit you and me. How startling to think that Jesus left heaven to become a single thread of life inside of Mary. Though

His birth was announced by angels and commemorated by the gifts of the Magi; He was also knit together in the same way as the rest of us. For nine months the Son of God let go of His home in heaven to be knit together as a man. He was slowly formed for nine months in Mary's womb until the day God finished His last stitch. Then He opened His eyes, took His first breath, and became God's knitting project given for the salvation of the world.

Day 19   God in Gift Wrapping

But made himself of no reputation, and took upon him the form of a servant, and was made in the likeness of men: And being found in fashion as a man, he humbled himself, and became obedient unto death, even the death of the cross.
Philippians 2:7-8 KJV

Sometimes I wonder who came up with the idea of gift wrapping? Why bother with ribbons and bows? I don't know about others, but I wrap gifts because I want them to be a surprise. So why would it be a strange thing that God came to us in gift wrapping? Since no one could see who Jesus was while wrapped in swaddling cloths, God sent angels to wake up shepherds to tell everyone about what was wrapped up in that manger!

And every Christmas we remember that on that special night in Bethlehem; at exactly the right moment, Jesus came as God in gift-wrapping, and by faith we have been opening God's gift of love in Christ ever since!

Day 20   Lentil Soup
And a Wise Man's Gift

And going into the house, they saw the child with Mary his mother, and they fell down and worshiped him. Then, opening their treasures, they offered him gifts, gold and frankincense and myrrh.
Matthew 2:11 ESV

"What's for dinner honey?" I said with a laugh knowing that it would be lentil soup for its third and final performance. During those first years of marriage, our food shopping was a low-cost adventure. So, with Christmas not far away; even putting up a tree with decorations was something we couldn't afford. That year, Christmas Eve was pay day and at four thirty I waited in line for my check. "Merry Christmas" My boss said winking as he handed me my envelope. "There's something extra in there for you tonight."

I peeked inside and drew a quick breath in astonishment. "Wow thanks Joe! Merry Christmas to you too" I said amazed at seeing a fifty-dollar bill tucked inside! I drove home through the heavy traffic getting there just before five. "Come on Nancy! Let's go buy a tree!" I shouted as I ran up the stairs to show her my bonus. Five minutes later we bundled up and drove to a Christmas tree lot where the owner was delighted to sell us a tree for five dollars, just before he closed. Then we raced over to the Woolworth store, where for ten cents each we bought some colored glass bulbs and a string of lights with tinsel. God didn't have to send the wise men with gifts to make it Christmas; but He did. That Christmas our wise man was named Joe and he left us a special gift on that Silent and Holy Night!

Day 21 What Can I Give to Him?

And to offer a sacrifice according to what is said in the Law of the Lord, "a pair of turtledoves, or two young pigeons." **Luke 2:24 ESV**

Yes, Mary and Joseph had heard from angels and watched shepherds and wise men kneel before Jesus. But when they came to the temple to dedicate God's miracle child, they offered only the sacrifice of the poorest of the poor. They were not ashamed to come to Herod's golden temple with their babe wrapped in swaddling clothes. They did not blush before the priest or feel ashamed in the company of the wealthy worshipers that day.

But why two turtledoves? Maybe God chose two doves so that they could come with something in each hand to give Him. Think how different it might have been if God had picked a princess or the daughter of a wealthy merchant. of Judea instead place of Mary. Instead, God chose a young peasant girl from Nazareth to be the mother of His Son. He specifically selected a poor village for Him to grow up in and a simple carpenter to provide Him a home. No place on earth was too humble for the Lord of the universe to visit and no offering too small for Him to treasure. So, if you wonder what you have to give; think of Mary with her turtledoves and then come with whatever you have in each hand.

Day 22   Our Small Part
in God's Gigantic Plan!

For he hath regarded the low estate of his handmaiden: for, behold, from henceforth all generations shall call me blessed. **Luke 1:48 KJV**

Forty-seven years ago, my wife and I packed our car with all we owned, squeezed our six-week-old son between boxes in the back seat and headed towards my grandparent's home a thousand miles away. Our plans were uncertain, and the failures that led us to that point made us feel that we were too small for even God to notice.

Joseph and Mary felt a bit like we did as they traveled with a donkey carrying a very pregnant Mary towards Judea. They had no promise of a place to live, no job for Joseph in Bethlehem and no certain plans for the future. But they traveled with hope because God had sent messages to Mary and Joseph that this was His plan, and they believed. Notice how today's verse says that God regarded Mary. He noticed her urgent need and took care of her. Today God also "regards" our low estate. He notices with great concern every single small detail of our lives. The baby son we carried in the back seat all those years ago is a father of teen-agers and is trusting Jesus for His own journey and, just as Mary and Joseph found out, we have learned what matters most is not how big we are, but that God has given us one small but special part in His gigantic plan!

Day 23   On This Day

For unto you is born this day in the city of David a Savior, who is Christ the Lord. **Luke 2:11 ESV**

As the shepherds drowsily watched their sheep, maybe they were thinking about what they would do in the morning with thoughts like: "I wonder if we need to buy bread?" - "Maybe we need to take our baby to the doctor" or even "I'm going to ask for a raise tomorrow!" Who knows what passed through their minds, as the lambs they were watching snuggled up under their mothers to sleep. Then suddenly, a big shining angel interrupted their daydreaming. What do you want to bet that those guys were terrified? But just before the shepherds could gather their wits enough to run like crazy, the angel calmed them with the words, "Do not be afraid." Then as they stood wondering what was going to happen next, God changed their plans forever with this message "This day," (even though it seemed like all the others before), "In the city of David" (their own hometown) "Is born…a Savior." (The one that generations of people had waited for)

Moments later they left behind their sheep, their plans and ran breathlessly to see the baby in the manger who came to rearrange their plans forever. If the God of the universe was interested in changing the plans of shepherds 2,000 years ago; why shouldn't He be interested in changing ours? So what plans are you making this year for Christmas? Would you leave everything to come running and see that on this day; right where you are Christ is still Lord just as the angel said?

Day 24 No Wallet - No cell phone
No keys!

And, lo, I am with you always, even
unto the end of the world. Amen. `
Matthew 28:20 KJV

Sometimes I like to go for a walk
without my cellphone, wallet, and keys.
It reminds me of my childhood when I
didn't have a wallet, because when I
needed money Mom would slip me a
quarter for the movies or a nickel for a
candy bar. Of course, we had no cell
phones, and house phones were reserved
for adults, except for saying, "Thanks
for the swell Christmas present Gramm"
and, "Gotta go. Here's mom." Maybe
most amazing of all, I had no keys,
because our house was never locked!
When we were out, sometimes the
neighbor even stopped in to borrow a
cup of sugar. Our lives were not perfect,
but we trusted that whatever we had was

enough. We depended on friends to get help if we got in trouble (which was often!) and we believed it was safe enough to leave the house unlocked because the bad guys had lost the war and now the good ones were in charge. And, though that world has disappeared, God's promises have not changed. He still knows exactly what we need and will take care of us. Even if our cell phones go dead, there is no place on earth where we need to ask, "Can you hear me now God?" The cross of Calvary has unlocked the door to God's house. He is watching and waiting for us with the assurance that we are welcome, we are expected, and that a place is set at Heaven's dinner table for all who will put their trust in Him!

Day 25
Hearts That Are Open to Him

To them God chose to make known how great among the Gentiles are the riches of the glory of this mystery, which is Christ in you, the hope of glory.
Colossians 1:27 ESV

There is an old Jamaican proverb that says, "Wise man rides donkey." that saying reminds me that real wisdom comes in the humble details of life. It is also interesting because Jesus was known for riding on donkeys. Of course the best-known occasion was when He rode into Jerusalem on Palm Sunday. But there was a far earlier time we might have forgotten. That was when Jesus rode for days, while safely tucked inside of Mary on her way to Bethlehem.

Most of us enjoy arriving at special events, decked out in our finest clothes, or pulling up to the curb in our newest car, but at Bethlehem, Jesus arrived by donkey and made His entrance where cattle were munching hay, chickens slept in the rafters and mice scurried back and forth in search of crumbs. He dressed in swaddling cloths, took his first nap in a barn, and was woken up by the joyful shouts of smelly shepherds. What wonderful news it is that He still comes even to our 21st century world to ordinary people riding on a donkey. So why not leave everything and kneel with the shepherds because He still comes for hearts that are looking for Him!

Day 26 Mary's Treasure

But Mary treasured up all these things
and pondered them in her heart.
Luke 2:19 NIV

I fumed in frustration as we sat on the
tarmac awaiting clearance for take-off. I
could see from my window two
mechanics working on the jet engine
hanging from the wing on my side of
the plane. It wasn't just the forty-five
minutes of waiting that bothered me but
also the realization that I was not in
control of my life. As Mary pulled the
blankets up around her hoping to get
some sleep while Jesus dozed in the
manger on that first Christmas night, we
would certainly have understood if she
had felt that way too. She had traveled
ninety miles by donkey while being nine
months pregnant. Then, after they
arrived in Bethlehem no one had any
room for them to stay, so she was forced
to give birth in a stable. Finally, just as

her newborn baby had settled down to sleep, a crowd of shepherds stampeded in and began singing and shouting something about angels. Wow what a night! Maybe some of us would have just simply broken down in tears at that point. But the Bible tells us that, Mary took time to think about all those things which, were entirely beyond her control and instead of complaining, she treasured them in her heart. Mary knew that everything that had happened that night was because God had promised a miracle child and she trusted that even though she wasn't in control: God was. She believed that regardless of how things looked; God was working everything for good. By the way, we had a safe flight; our plane still landed right on time and God taught me that every day is a treasure when we trust in His control.

Day 27   The Wise Men's Faith

And going into the house they saw the
child with Mary His mother and they
fell down and worshipped Him. Then
opening their treasures, they offered
Him gifts, gold and frankincense and
myrrh. **Matthew 2:11 ESV**

What had the wise men come to see? If
it was the child of a king; why hadn't he
been in Herod's palace? If He were a
great leader, then where were His
armies and the earthly power of his
family? As the Magi came to the final
stop on their star-led journey maybe
these questions still coursed through
their minds. Instead of any of the places
they had imagined they would discover
Him, they found themselves standing
inside a simple village home. His
parents were neither rich nor
impressive. In fact, Joseph and Mary
were not even on the ruling council of
the unimpressive village of Bethlehem.

But the wise men knew there could be no mistaking the miracle of the star which had appeared to them and led them safely on their journey. There could be no confusion because their search had been confirmed by an ancient prophecy that God's chosen Messiah was to be born in Bethlehem. They had no more doubts because in the end the star stopped and stood directly over only one doorway. Surely this child for whom even stars in the sky were directed was even greater than a king. He must be deserving not only of their earthly treasures, but also of their worship and their very lives. Like us they were strangers, but they had come by faith and in His mercy God was delighted to show them His Son!

Day 28   A Walk in the Park

Behold, a virgin shall be with child, and shall bring forth a son, and they shall call his name Emmanuel, which being interpreted is, God with us.
Matthew 1:23 KJV

Today's world overflows with activities and non-stop media, so just going for a walk seems pretty humdrum. But today's verse tells us that Jesus came to earth because God just wanted to be with us. Now that may not sound exciting to you, but I have found that when I ask our grandkids.

"Who wants to go to the park?"

An enthusiastic answer, "I do!" rings out!

They want to go because it means that Poppy will push them on the swings, chase them around the jungle gym and help them reach the water fountain.

Even more important than the things we do is our conversation along the way. I love to tell them stories of when I was a kid, getting soaking wet while catching frogs or buying candy bars for a nickel. Jesus lived, died, and was raised from the dead, not just so He could be the big shot of the universe, but because God wanted to be Emmanuel – (God with us). Just as our grandchildren understand what it means to be a part of our family, by walking with me, so we learn what it means to be a Christian by walking with Jesus, Remember that it took three years of walking with His disciples, for Jesus to teach them how to follow Him. His miracles were impressive, but it was while walking through a field and munching on corn, that He taught His them about the Sabbath. Walking to a party at Matthew's house He showed them that God loved sinners and when Jesus walked out into the country to pray, His disciples asked, "Lord, teach us to pray." On His last day on earth, Jesus walked with thieves to the cross, then three days later He walked out to meet with Mary Magdalene. Everything God wants to do in our hearts, He will do if we are ready to walk with Him. He is called Emmanuel – God With Us_ and this Christmas He wants to go for a walk with you!

Day 29 God's Gift

For the wages of sin is death but the gift of God is eternal life, through Jesus Christ our Lord. **Romans 6:23 KJV**

At Fort Knox in Kentucky the U.S. government stores over nine million pounds of gold bullion. As you can imagine this is one of the most secure facilities anywhere on the planet. That gold has been there for over ninety years. Nothing more has gone in, and nothing has been taken out. That is the way things are with the treasures of this life. They are kept under lock and key and rarely used. But at the birth of Jesus Christ on Christmas everything was changed by a treasure that was given away. In fact, the entire Christmas story is about that gift. When all is said and sung about Joseph and Mary, the shepherds and wise men, there would be nothing worth celebrating were it not for the baby in the manger. This Christmas:

whether you sit alone or are surrounded by family; remember that God has included you on His gift list. When His first smile lit up the dark stable it streaked across our own sky like daybreak shattering the darkness of a coal black sky. All our light displays, family gatherings and candlelight services would be worthless were it not for Him. In a hundred years everything we own, and all our human accomplishments will disappear, and the only thing that will count is if we have received God's gift. Why not pray right now and ask to receive that treasure of eternal life through Jesus Christ our Lord?

Day 30   Jesus is Still Seeking You!

Ask, and it shall be given you; seek, and ye shall find; knock, and it shall be opened unto you: **Matthew 7:7 KJV**

The Magi followed the Christmas Star, hoping to find a king. Shepherds hurried down dark hillside paths seeking the Messiah. Mary and Joseph wearily knocked on every door desperately asking for a place for their child to be born. Someone else also came seeking that night, and that person was God himself. As He opened His eyes, Jesus came looking for you and me. So this year as our Christmas journey ends let's pause and ask ourselves whether the greatest seeker of all has found what He was looking for. His knocking at the door of our hearts echoes with each hammer stroke on the nails of the cross. But will we hear and answer His knock, or will we allow ourselves to be deafened by the noise and the busyness of life? Jesus has been seeking you and me since He lay in the manger two thousand years ago. Whether you are surrounded by family with all the trimmings of the holiday or are alone in a hotel room or a prison, God loved you enough to come looking for you. Will this Christmas be the day you are found? Why not kneel with shepherds and wise men with this as your Christmas prayer?

"Lord Jesus I thank you for seeking for me and for your sacrifice on the cross for my sins. Forgive me for all my selfishness and the hurt that I have caused. Come into my heart and find me today!"

Merry Christmas! May all the blessings of being found by Jesus Christ be yours for now and forever – Amen!

And a New Year Lies Ahead

And now the year has passed my child
See the new one lies ahead
Yes all those days both sad and sweet
Have slipped into their beds

To sleep until the hour God sets
For eyes to open wide
And see His sunlight streaming in
To spread our wings and fly!

Is Jesus the Author of Your Story?

Now some of you may wonder where all the little stories in this Christmas book come from. But have you ever stopped to realize that all of us have a story to tell - (though thankfully most of them never end on paper!) Stories help us to understand, in ways that simple explanations simply leave us feeling like we have a 1,000-piece puzzle to complete or just another set of facts to memorize. But when Jesus was born, the Bible tell us that He was God's Word, made flesh. A simpler way of saying that might be to say that Jesus was God's story come to life. Jesus came to be the story of God's love, as well as His holiness: God's mercy as well as His truth. Most importantly, the story of Jesus is God's gift for anyone willing to listen and believe. Jesus is also God's story who has come to live in our hearts if we will receive Him as our Lord and Savior. At that very moment, the greatest miracle of all occurs: Jesus becomes the author of our faith. When He puts His name on the cover of our heart, then He includes us His best-selling story book of all time: The Book of Life!

The following pages are included to give you a space to stop for a moment and think of one of your favorite Christmas stories. Just taking the time to write them down will give a chance for your family and friends to read some of what God has written in your hearts over the years. There is no one right story. It only depends on what God has done in your life and what that means to you!

My Christmas Story

_____

_____

_____

Name:

Date:

About the Author - Nancy and I are getting ready to celebrate 50 wonderful and crazy years together. We have two sons, six lively grandsons and one wonderful granddaughter! I love to write about nursing home ministry, as well as practical devotionals, poetry and even a few songs.

Other Devotional Resources

Thank you for sharing your Christmas with me. If this devotional has been a blessing to you, here are some other resources you might like, available in both eBook and paperback from Kindle Direct Publishing (KDP) @ Amazon.com.

The Joy of Easter is a daily reader that begins on Ash Wednesday and continues through Easter Sunday. Each day shares a verse a story and a call to consider how Jesus calls us to live out the joy of our faith today.

Grace For the Road is a 40-day devotional especially for caregivers. We, our loved ones along with volunteers and staff  form a special community with a unique way of seeing the world. These readings are messages of the grace that God offers us; when we reach out to touch the hem of His garment.

Made in the USA
Columbia, SC
01 December 2024

47997876R00043